THE JEREMIAD
Christian Homesteaders Gazette

QUARTERLY SCHOLARLY REPORTS, ESSAYS, DEVOTIONALS & HUMOR, COMPILED FOR THE PRAXEOLOGION OF THE GREAT
• TRADITIONAL ANGLICAN CHURCH OF AMERICA •

VOLUME 3 • ISSUE No. 1 • AUTUMN, 2023

MATTEAWAN MARY GETS UPSET WITH VINNIE, THE KINDLY CORRECTIONS OFFICER! P. 35

!&#@!!#!!@

I0106489

$10.00
ISBN 979-8-9889300-2-0
51000>
9 798988 930020

FR. MIKE D. LEARNS STOCHASTIC PROBABILITY VIA HIS WHACKY ITALIAN GHOST-HUNTER COUSIN! P. 1

The Brazen Bull of Stochastic Probability
By Fr. Mike DellaVecchia

When I was twenty years old, my father and I visited a town in the Province of Caserta, in Italy.

This hilly corner of the Campania contained the ruins of a Medieval castle. The town was Gioia Sannitica.

The lady at the souvenir shop at our hotel in Rome, who spoke fluent English, told me what my grandfather had always told me. It was that the name of the town, when translated into English, was "Joyous Saints."

Gramps had also told me, "DellaVecchia's have always come from this place."

This rural hamlet is where I would meet my third cousins. My father and I arrived there in the early afternoon on a sunny Thursday in March. The woman at the front of the gray house with the white door dropped her rake when she heard my father say her last name. Her name was Rosa.

Her eyes opened wide and her mouth fell open and she screamed into the house for her family to come out and she ran to us and yanked at my father's arms to come out and be hugged. We were now surrounded by many people dragging us inside, holding our hands, hugging us, kissing our cheeks.

I was excited to get to know my twenty—maybe forty—cousins, sweet laughing people all full of Life. I was given tours of their two red-tiled roof homes and small farms.

First, a barn with a rustic apartment with a chamber pot up top, with its low-sloping bronze green roof, where we were offered to sleep but Dad said we couldn't. The main house with its large living room and oversized kitchen, one and a half floors and a root-cellar, a stable with bovine, a tobacco-curing shed, and a small

1

plantation outback. The front yard and side drive, all virgin gravel wrapping around toward an old metal incinerator that was shared by the other low-rise house with its own shed and barn, and a slate-walled water well, and a tiny bakehouse, and a citrus garden, and another driveway with pillars to hook up cattle, and several overfed mongrels skulking around on patrol, quiet and sniffing everyone, descending and ascending the gravel footpath that led to another entrance to Via Colle.

On this day I would be handed cup after cup of homemade red and white wine and cheese in the living room. Cugine everywhere, some of them not really cousins but jumping in and out of the houses as if they had always lived there.

Young men clad in plaid shirts and denim from America, the pant legs and sleeves always too long. Robust girls with thick wrists and ankles and rosy cheeks in print dresses, white socks, and tough saddle shoes sitting on the arm rests or cushions of homemade and antique worn furniture.

Beautiful tan young ladies named Maria and Angela and Anna and Cristina and Lina and Gianna, the wives and daughters dressed in work clothes and the older single women and widows dressed like 1950s movie stars but looking with grins only at the floor.

All the men at the far walls overlooking everybody, never walking, and making wise cracks at all the movers and runners and chatterboxes and trouble-makers and little bigshots—the fussing females and the children and the dogs and cats. The sunlight that poured through the windows blinked into dazzling signals of life that broke through it every second.

Old men with canes and old women in kerchiefs that they pulled down halfway amid their scalps sat underneath the four big yellow hanging sacks of formaggio and black iron pots in the kitchen and clutched cups of wine and black coffee and lemony water and all the younger ladies were looking at me and were saying silly secret things quietly to each other in Italian and giggling and then gesturing softly at my dad and some of them shrugging and then looking back at me again.

My father and I accepted the sudden invitation of the eldest DellaVecchia to go on a walk with him. "Later, not-a now," he promised.

"Later?" asked Dad.

"Yeah, you come-a with-a me, later," Angelo assured Dad.

Here was a loud 57-year-old man with his top two buttons undone to exhibit his wire-haired chest, his harmless braggadocio blaring beneath brown-tanned skin, and a full head of grey-streaked rooster black hair pulled backwards, and several missing frontal and side teeth in his constant smile that tried hard to seem somehow menacing, and a lean laborer's build. He was happy but he let you know that he did not want to appear happy, but instead powerful and feared and strong and always in control, so long as his wife ran everything. He just knew that he *knew* that he *knew* that he was content, but you could also tell that he was always working so that he could earn his happiness. He was acting the part of supreme authority, the local man who knew everything and who ran everything everywhere, probably even the planets up yonder. Italy, to me, was a place that let a man, even a cocky everyday man, just be a man.

It was explained to us by his wife Rosa that he wanted us to venture off with him, to walk uphill on a trail through the woods, to visit the old castle.

"Something tells me we had better do as Angelo says," answered my Dad laughing. Now, Angelo knew Dad had said this but nodded hard and he laughed, too.

Among all my cousins, Angelo was also appearing to be the most excited to host our visit, because of how our presence as his "wealthy" American cousins appeared to upgrade his social standing.

We were certain that after my father had already given Rosa £1,372, the equivalent of a thousand U.S. dollars, he was not interested in anything other than showing us off. Dad was never expecting to stay long, but this couple insisted that we should.

Giving his family time to prepare food for us, he hurried us into the little village. This gave all these cugini the time to pile into the houses and give us grand tours.

Although the local cafoni and Carabinieri were very polite, it was clear they regarded Angelo as something of a madman. Angelo was always drinking too much, often getting into arguments, and telling his infamous tall tales that were either meant to forestall a creditor, or, to excuse his wintertime absence from a Switzerland-bound agriculture team. Or, they were just intended to impress giggly young ladies.

One time, said a dairy hauler, a carabinieri had to arrest a foreman who was chasing Angelo around the village with a shovel because he had "borrowed" a dump truck to rescue his daughters from a UFO!

My father and I had during the late morning been sitting and laughjng along on bar stools drinking Ouzo at Osteria Via Nocito but we were warned with albeit-respectful winks and smirks by the men drinking here not to accept any "schemi veloci" from our cousin.

I do not know how my father knew that this term meant, "fast schemes," but Dad had been around old-world Italians in Brooklyn all his life and he did appear to enjoy all this attention.

Even Angelo, who did seem concerned about what the cafoni were telling my dad about him, appeared to appreciate how our presence there was making everyone feel. My dad, glad that it had become lunch hour, paid the bar tab for about twenty people. Angelo now leered over at every one of them, as if expecting them automatically to elect him for mayor.

4

After lunch surrounded by his immediate family (and the the tons of people who filed into the house), we realized that Angelo was nonetheless merely (or most often *was*) a lovable well-healed rake, his eyes never sent away from his family.

His five children, three boys and two girls, adored him, always holding onto his arms or dragging his eyes and ears toward their attention.

He announced to everybody that he was about to take us on a walk and that they should stay in the house. So we walked outside and Dad dragged me away from all the ladies who gave me many goodbyes and shook my hand and grabbed my sleeve as I left them behind.

Angelo puffed out his chest and he leaned his forearm over the gate of his small tobacco plantation during our exit from his property, to show it off to us, and he also showed us where he kept pigs, and had five cows and a bull and where the family made their own cheese, olive oil, and wine and how they did not ever need to go into Naples for groceries but confessed that the men had to go into Switzerland for work every winter.

Angelo was also known to have a notorious following among the embarrassed parents of the town's teenagers. The youth got their first cigarettes or liquor from him—given these gifts provided, as we were so-warned back at the bar—that the youngsters would come away with him into the fields behind their Caselle neighborhood whenever the Sun went down behind the Matese Mountains to help him with his work. They would help him and his kids watch for UFOs! This was a man who never ever wanted to be alone.

Sometimes, Angelo told us, the ghost of Spartacus could be seen skulking behind the juniper and oak trees of the southwest slope overlooking Via Colle. As if its originator had just lost the Third Servile War, the apparition was said to descend down an overgrown southwest-Appenenine trail during twilight on Tuesdays, trying to find the Volturno River, in his escape from General Crassus, to reach the Mediterranean, where Cilician pirates would smuggle him to Sicily.

Angelo also presented to us the permanently locked stone house that my great-great grandfather had built just twenty feet from his home, a two-story house made of bare stones without ivory or moss, covered in long oak wood slates, its foundation made of small boulders impacted into the clay soil and the tough brown grass. Nobody had opened the door in a decade because, as Angelo told us, it was said that opening its door would compromise the setting of its lintel and the house would resultantly come tumbling down.

In the late twentieth century, many Italians left Italy for places such as Ireland, the United Kingdom, Canada, or the U.S., escaping the reforms of the socialist takeover of King Victor Emanuel and his son, Umberto I. For them, the Marxists were worse than the Nazis. And, by the 1920s, Benito Mussolini, who forced the people of Campania into state labor, refused to allow anyone to leave the peninsula.

"But-that a-Hitler, he was not-a so bad-a guy, that Hitler guy-a," said Angelo, who added, "Adolfo, he not-a make us fight-a when-a we no longer said-a we aint gonna fight-a for him no more, so too badda for him and we stay at home and wes milk-a the cow!" He blew a raspberry up into the air as we walked away from the "Casa Vecchia-DellaVecchia" back into the main house.

The DellaVecchia's who had left Gioia Sannitica in 1899 settled in Hamden and New Haven, Connecticut. My father was born in Hamden in 1934. His father found the address of these cugini again in 1981 and visited there in 1982. They did not have a phone and had to return his calls from the Western Union office in the town. Gramps slept for a week in the barn apartment during his visit and now it was our turn to meet everybody, in 1988.

I had been having the time of my life and even got a wedding proposal from my timid teenaged cousin, Lina, via her outspoken mother, Rosa. I turned the offer down, because I had been previously warned to expect the proposal in a whispered aside by my father.

Dad had figured out why Lina was suddenly dressed like an angel in white lace and, looking like a beautiful drink of milk inside a table doily, she had served all the lunchtime food, although Dad was meanwhile admonishing me while I drank about a quart-load of their red wine, "We do not have the money to get Lina to America and pay a dowry, so forget about marrying your third cousin, Lina."

Dad was also noting that, because the humors of the big man's eyes were yellow, Angelo was obviously stricken with liver disease. Pop advised that we ought to accept Angelo's invitation to go on a walk with him, to leave our other cugini behind and follow the man to the highest point in Caselle, to visit the castle, because we were probably seeing our cousin during his last days.

We walked out along the gravel dog path onto a pebbled cutaway beneath trellises of grape vines alongside a row of halved wooden barrels of young almond and date bushes in soil. It was mid-afternoon by now and I drunkenly asked if we were walking to see the ghost of Spartacus.

"Non vedremo Spartaco!" came the chuckling response from a younger man, who ran up just behind us named Franco, a non-blood relation, a house painter who had married one of our cousins. He was informing us that Spartacus's ghost would not appear on the roster that evening. He had his eyes on a road cutoff up ahead.

Franco darted past as we walked along the Via Colle and we watched him trudge up an old logging trail by himself with what appeared to be two cans of paint. He was suddenly followed uphill by teens, who had just come out of their hiding places in the brush, wearing Metallica and Slayer jackets, smoking cigarettes.

7

"Franco gives them their cigarettes," said my dad to me quietly. I wondered how he could have known this.

"No, no," said Angelo. "Franco, naw, he just gone uppa the hill so he can maybe paint-a somebody house-a," explained Angelo.

"Sure, I'll just bet he did," said my father, upon which Angelo boldly winked at me and I laughed aloud.

We were passing many fields of trees and bushes in spring bloom—Melanurca apple and Cilento-fig trees jumping out of scrubby volcanic fields that form the low ridges exposed to direct sun, white citrus blossoms budding in rich olive groves with broken rusty iron fences, with green and yellow colors sensed like smells in the body, so beautiful I felt as if I did not ever want to go home to Brooklyn, New York. The sweet odor of wine, and the enchanting aroma of tobacco leaves coming from everywhere, and the unexpected flavor of chocolate *tasted* as a smell coming from stucco-encrusted homes just yards from the edge of the road. Antique browned machines of war and labor, canons and tanks and steam shovels, stranded and rusting in the fields and covered with old graffiti and many children jumping from them onto the brush on the sandy soil. The salty maddening wind from the Tyrrhenian Sea sent dozens of miles over the Pozzuoli harbor that had brushed over the sprawl of Naples, collecting the scent of formaggio and candy and dirty concrete and ancient sewers and oil painting, all of it coming across the Campania to this very road and dropping its "contents" whenever the wind stopped and strangely seemed to turn back to the sea after knocking into the white image of the castle way at the top of hill we were ascending.

I did not know the history of the mysterious Castello di Gioia Sannitica except that it was built by the Lombards. We were on a four-mile hike up the Via Caselle. My dad said it was good for me to "work off that wine."

"Ha un fantasma!" said Angelo. I could have sworn that Angelo had just said the name of the 1979 Don Coscarelli horror film, but I saw my father flipping, concerned, through his Berlitz translation book.

"That place is haunted by a ghost?" Dad asked.

"Sì, questo fantasma è un dolore nel culo!" More flipping sounds now came from Dad on his Berlitz book.

But I figured out what Angelo meant by how he rolled his eyes and gestured as if he were angry at a woman. "She drive-a me pazzo!"

"'Pazzo' means crazy," said Dad.

"Is the ghost a lady or a man?" I asked.

"The ghosta? She a bigga fatta lady and she a bigga pain in my uh abbondanza!" (He didn't actually say "abbondanza"). I was now roaring with laughter. Angelo began talking without a breath in Italian, saying strings of words about how he apparently hated the ghost and that "she" had done many annoying things to him but that he did not know how to get rid of her.

There is a lot you can understand when you experience a person speaking in a foreign language by watching his face, hearing him talk in a high-pitched voice like a lady who nags him and groans in ghostly wails, and seeing him shrug as if there was just nothing he could do about her.

"For crying out loud, we could have gone to see the Aqueduct today," said Dad.

Pop muttered something to the effect of *how* he could have *ever* taken me on this hike, etcetera, etcetera, pinching his brow in his fingers, walking onward, darting his eyes around the trees.

Thanking Dad for letting us take this trip I could not take my eyes off of him (being merely that I utterly loved my father), while Angelo spoke in broken English and sometimes uttered long strings of self-amused Italian, probable idiomatic expressions,

9

some of it surely curse words. When you are still young enough to idolize your own dad, you are amazed at how "they" (*i.e.,* dads) just seem to know in advance everything that is bound to happen.

"Dad, just what *exactly* are we going up there to see, at that Castle?" Dad laughed and rolled his eyes as Angelo broke in.

"She drive me crazy every night. You gotta see this a thing-a. She got a bigga mouth!" said Angelo.

My father, now folding his hands as he walked, put one hand in the air to wave to Angelo to just to keep on walking.

"Give me a second, Mike," said Dad. "What a bunch of bull crap," I heard Dad say.

I knew that *if* Pop had not already figured out what was going on, he would have pulled us away, back toward the house. The truth could never have been all that bad, because here was Pop merely shaking his head, holding back a laugh but also staring into space telling me to let him be the one to tell this tale to my mom.

"No, seriously, what's going on, Dad?" Dad opened his mouth to take a breath before he spoke but closed his mouth just as quickly.

Instead, Angelo was talking and talking and now pointing at the trees and the sky (probably saying things about UFOs and ghosts and comets), and then he suddenly stopped right before Dad finally answered my question and told us about how the ghost had once helped him fix his car on the way home from Naples.

Angelo spewed out loud Italian words very rapidly, while he pantomimed driving a car, and wiped imaginary sweat away from his forehead, and finally indicated that there was a bigga car accident. Finally, he mimed that a ghost came flying to his wreck from midair, went right to work on his Fiat, and fixed his car "right good-a."

"OK, so the ghost fixes cars, does she now?" Dad asked him.

"She crazy but she pretty nice, my ghost-a! You gonna see her so you be nice-a!"

Dad face palmed and finally explained to me that this was Angelo's way of paying us back for the £1,372 gift.

"Angelo sent his brother-in-law Franco up the hill ahead of us with those kids to go pull off a stunt," he said

"What kind of stunt?" I asked.

"I think they are all going to dress up as ghosts," Dad explained. "Or at least Franco is."

Just then, five of the kids came running down the Via Caselle, clutching boxes of cigarettes. They said "Grazie!" to Angelo.

"So, Cousin Angelo bought all the teenagers cigarettes with the £1,372?" I asked.

"I hope not all of it," Dad said. Angelo shot Dad a hard smirky look as if to say that the money was *his* to spend as he liked. Apparently, he had sneaked it out of wherever his wife had stashed it.

"This better be good, Cugine!" Dad yelled.

"Oh, you gonna like it a lot!" answered Angelo.

Finally entering the frontal precincts of the castle, Angelo stopped talking. We passed through the ruptured walls of stables, holding our balance on tan metamorphic stones and flat boulders that formed into steps, passing up a winding causeway toward the outer courtyard where colonnades now lay in fragmented marble pieces in the adjoining patches of grass. Angelo led us through the inner courtyard, where we stepped cross the scattered pieces of the stone curtain, stepping into the remains of the tower and the keep, across the sun-bleached slates of the bailey, and walked through the granite chunks of the corps de logis, and the rusty iron bars of the collapsed gatehouse and over the fallen stones of portcullis, out to the fortress areas. We strode along the igneous walkway that spilled into the apartments area and looked over the wrecked homes and shops of a long-dead community. Angelo was walking fast but tolerated our request to take pictures with Dad's new drug-store Minolta 35-mm camera, or to view something through my binoculars.

"What is that shiny thing way at the end of the fortress?" I was pointing in the direction of the a partially fallen rampart. A metallic plate was reflecting the last bit of daylight our way through one of the preserved battlements.

"We go look at that now, come on," Angelo said.

Stepping down a beige shale staircase to a split level that was eight feet lower, we stepped off the slates and hopped across the fallen stones of the southwest rampart of the fortress. We walked along the five-to-eight foot sections of the wall. The sunlight on the metal ahead bristled out yellow rays that suggested it was made of brass or bronze.

"Come in-a here with me," said Angelo, and we followed him as he turned at the left corner of the broken southwest turret onto lines and piles of schist bricks that just barely betrayed images of right angles which indicated outlines of soldier apartments.

"Look-a down-a now, boys!" Angelo ordered.

We threw our gaze down toward a patio, reached by a volcanic-rock ramp that we sometimes needed to slide down on our buttocks, to offload ourselves onto a cleared piazza.

"Dad, I saw something like this in slides in my art history class."

"Well, I can't believe people put this down here," said Dad. He never wanted to hear about my art studies. He had thrown me a

12

bone by taking me on this sales trip with his company. I had spent all day walking around the Vatican museum with him a day earlier. However, this was a working-class man, who could not understand how I had talked him into allowing me to major in art. I always used to tell him, "It's because you taught me how to be a good salesman, Dad."

This lower level was formed by a much older positioning of slabs of impacted diabase, suggesting that the castle and fortress had been built on top of this very ancient level.

"We are in the middle of the remains of a temple, Pop."

In the back of the piazza was a six-foot-high bronze bull. It stood ten or fifteen feet from the remains of a shale wall.

"Moooooo!" bleated Angelo.

"This is a hunk of bull, alright!" Dad said.

If Angelo was not being such a hilarious cut-up we might have otherwise have been scared.

Meanwhile, our manic cousin was shoving broken sticks underneath the bull. Teenagers came out from behind the wall and said nothing but smoked their cigarettes and put more sticks underneath the bull. They lit the sticks with lighters that they removed from their jeans. I remember asking one of the female members if Angelo had bought her her jeans, which were a rare item in the 1980s and she gladly said he did.

My father meanwhile had walked around the wall and saw a road leading back to the Via Casella and a Carabinieri officer writing down things in a leather-bound pad, talking to a couple of the young Italian metalheads. My dad's mouth was dropped open because everywhere he looked were things made of bronze—roof sections, fountain parts, drain pipes and gutters, arms of old statues, street lamps—with some of the oxidation brushed away, but most of it greener than Ireland. The metal plate that rose above

13

the wall that we had seen earlier, which Angelo had been brushing to make it appear fresh again, was now reflecting the dim dusk. Angelo was running a scrap-metal business.

The region was full of bronze, brass, and copper discarded articles, and Angelo was making book here. Another wall that was perpendicular to this one, partially concealed a three-wall shed, in which sat a moonshine still.

The Carabinieri officer was writing all this down. During the 1940s, moonshine had become illegal. Angelo had a still. Its hoses were made of copper and were thus as green as clover but its boiler was made of bronze, an alloy which oxidizes at a darker shade of green.

Suddenly Angelo ran over to the officer while reaching into his pocket and gave him the rest of the money my dad had given him. It was pay-off time in the Campania. My father, dumbfounded, stared at the officer to make sure he had gotten enough cash, with my father counting aloud the twenties that were placed, one by one, into the officer's palm, and then we all watched him drive away.

"So I just paid that piece of trash £900."

"She's a worth it, you gonna see," said Angelo, who neither appeared as promising nor as enthusiastic, suddenly.

Just then, screaming was heard coming from inside the bull. The fire was well under way.

"Here she comes!" Angelo announced. "Come on ova here-a and we exorcise this bull-a."

"Oh, no, please tell me nobody is inside that statue," said Pop.

"You gonna get outta here, you sonovabeecha inna the name-a Santa Maria, you stupid-a beecha!" yelled Angelo at the bull.

14

Dad did not know things would get this far. But he could have probably put it on a short list. He stood next to me to make sure nothing happened to me even though I was already taller and stronger than him. Angelo was screaming at the bull.

"And you leave-a our farm all alone, you stupid bigga shotta, you!" Angelo was now furiously hitting the bull with a stick, shouting at it in Italian.

"Vafancullo! Tu e un rompipale!" These are expressions that should not ever be Googled.

The screaming grew more fierce inside the bronze beast as the fire raged.

Just then a chamber on the "belly" side of the statue was revealed by one of the Metalheads, who pulled aside a clasp to unfasten its door. Out poked Franco's hysterical face and then out came the rest of him.

We got closer to the man, hoping to help him, only to notice that the fire had not been built close enough to the bull to cause Franco to get scorched, but that the sticks had been safely separated from away it.

"Stupid idiots," said Dad.

Franco, who was wearing a woman's blonde wig and was wearing painter's togs that were painted flourescent green, finally jumped out of the bull and ran across the piazza while Angelo and the kids took turns beating the hysterical transvestite with sticks, tumbling out across the piazza in the early moonlight, then up the steps, across the bailey and out the temple entrance, through the fallen stones of the corps de logis, toward the Via Caselle.

Five pre-teens dressed in flourescent green painters togs "flew" around the piazza, howling—some of them smoking cigarettes—and causing my father to nod his head in acceptance of what he was just put through.

"These must be the ghosts!" I exclaimed, laughing hard at everything that was going on.

"You like-a this?" Angelo asked us.

"Sure, it's fine ya nutjob," Dad managed, trying not to appear furious.

"No, you you like-a this, cugine?" Angelo repeated.

"Really, I get it," Dad answered, then said more quietly, "Stupid idiots."

The Metalheads, three or four of them who were too cool to join in the drama, were guffaw and then falling against each other, holding their wheezing chortles up their noses, pointing at my father, puffing on their butts, and seeing how my dad was now shaking his head in disbelief. They threw anything they could into the fire now, including strips of bronze, which, when burned emitted a foul odor, which sent Angelo through the roof, so to speak. Angelo ran back to the fire and kicked the kids out of the piazza and started kicking the fire down to its embers and scraping the smokey bottoms of his shoes on the slate floor. The smell was so bad that Pop was pinching his nostrils together.

"I can't believe I came to Italy." Dad was now sitting on a boulder laughing to himself. He could not stop. These were belly laughs that I always enjoyed when I was a child, watching Daffy Duck abuser Elmer Fudd on the television. What was the harm here, anyway? Was utility not served? These were more innocent times, if not being a profane side show taking place within the mere foothills of a near Apocalypse.

At least Angelo had a workforce that served a variety of community needs. The kids got paid for finding the scrap. Meanwhile all the kids, the preteens included, were being babysat by Angelo and by Franco, and by the older teens, so that many parents could work during the day. Angelo had many customers, especially the police.

16

It was all very demented. But I considered the whole racket to be incredibly entertaining and, what, with my being twenty and all, well, I wanted to stay here forever.

"Italy is awesome, Dad!"

On the way back to the house in Angelo's car (his Fiat had been parked by Franco behind the wall), Dad explained to me that Angelo was the "entertainment" for the tourists who visit the castle. Usually the "shows" end up being "better" (presumably) but we had basically dropped in on the family that morning after all. We had not told them we were visiting them. The Carabineri in the town center had to give us directions to the house.

"We do it better next time," said Angelo, who added, "but you are so special so we hadda give up the space-a-ship show," said Angelo. Understandably, the UFO gig on Tuesdays was a lesser event. Angelo's crew had just been given a commission to do the "Brazen Bull" show. Dad added:

"And on the side, he has a scrap metal business and he apparently pays off the cops every week," Pop explained. Angelo also wanted me to marry his daughter and convince my dad to invest as a partner in his scrap-metal business.

When we got back to the house, Lina, her love remaining unrequited by my arrogant heart, was seated on the couch crying, being comforted by Rosa, her mother. Rosa shot up from the couch and dragged him into the kitchen by the canvas fabric of his shirt's shoulder. She was screaming at him in the kitchen now, in Italian. Her man had found the stash of money.

Although the family was poor, and the father was a hustler, all the men had wrist watches, because they were line workers and farm helpers during the day. They were all glancing at their watches now. We said our goodbyes and all the hugs and the cheek kisses were so powerful that I can still feel them these 35 years later.

17

My father hugged Rosa and put some more Liras into cash into her hand but he did not ever tell me how much he had given her. It is better that some words never reach the air, lest Satan overhear them and, in this case, plant a new idea in Angelo's head, or so I figured.

It should also be mentioned that before we had left the castle scrap yard, that there was another device that Angelo had showed us.

This piece was a type of boiler that was roughed into concrete backfills at the base of the lowest part of the granite wall in the piazza. It was an Aeolipile. The boiler was the same kind as the one in the still.

Two bronze pipes extended out of this tank, and a third, located in the column rising from it, was a shaft that fed into a rotating unit which was inserted upon an axis. My dad said it was some kind of a heating implement for the castle. Angelo told us that it had sat here on the lower level and that he had found it beneath the stones twenty years earlier. It had been part of the much older temple, not the castle. I made the upper part spin with my hands after Angelo demonstrated how. It too was made of bronze.

Pondering the Aeolipile all during his life is probably what kept Angelo coming back to the castle and starting a business there (and he did actually give the teenagers cash as well as cigarettes). The desire for truth inspires not merely magnetivity toward the source, but various peripheral motivations, such as when the lover of classical architecture, such as the carpenter William H. Reynolds, builds an amusement park—such as Dreamland in Coney Island in 1904—featuring a re-creation of the Roman Forum, because he is amazed with the "golden-section" proportion of rectangles. Angelo was thus collecting antiques because it helped him to understand where he was living as a citizen of an ancient land and to imagine how he and his family fit into the history, if only just to keep it animated for spectators.

What I am about to tell you are things that I could never have known back then. Certainly, I enjoyed my access to all the libraries of New York City I could ever hope to walk into; and, so it was not the Internet of today that led me to an understanding of what I had observed then: There is indeed a supernatural "dimension" about which people are discernibly aware. As a father, my father's love gave him Spiritual Discernment. This only arrives through Faith and is why good fathers will protect and support their homes while teaching their sons about how to survive. Meanwhile, ambitious men such as Angelo, invent machines or develop weird means to help them cope with evils they cannot use their will to overcome. I was in the presence of something that needed collateral definition, a spectacle wrought by a madman, a distant cousin of mine, in the twilight of an Italian countryside.

What in Heaven's name was an Aeolipile?

Much later in this book, an Appendix will give definitions written by ancient and antiquated authors for it, and as regards related mechanisms. Here are the words of Hero of Alexandria, about his formulation of a concept for this steam-driven device written by Marcus Vitruvius Pollio:

"Place a cauldron over a fire: a ball shall revolve on a pivot. A fire is lighted under a cauldron... containing water, and covered at the mouth by the lid... With this the bent tube... communicates, the extremity of the tube being fitted into a hollow ball... Opposite to the extremity... place a pivot... resting on the lid... and let the ball contain two bent pipes, communicating with it at the opposite extremities of a diameter, and bent in opposite directions, the bends being at right angles and across the lines... As the cauldron gets hot it will be found that the steam, entering the ball through... passes out through the bent tubes towards the lid, and causes the ball to revolve, as in the case of the dancing figures (The Pneumatics; Hero of Alexandria; Sec. 50: "The Steam Engine"; A.D. 70).

These complicated instructions (the ellipses above replace the letters referring to the diagrams that Hero had drawn), were based on the following theory by Pollio:

19

"Æolipylæ are hollow brazen vessels, which have an opening or mouth of small size, by means of which they can be filled with water. Previous to the water being heated over the fire, but little wind is emitted, as soon, however, as the water begins to boil, a violent wind issues forth. Thus a simple experiment enables us to ascertain and determine the causes and effects of the great operations of the heavens and the winds" *(de Architectura;* Marcus Vitruvius Pollio; Book I; Chap. 6; B.C. 15).

My father, Angelo, and myself were the last people to leave the piazza. Or, so we thought. Somebody had crept inside the bull again and was howling like a ghost. But Angelo was not laughing as he drove the tiny Fiat but my father and I were giggling—my father, more from sheer exhaustion. Angelo told us the real occupant of the bull was the "real ghost." Or, "Il fantasma reale."

My father winked at me. However, Angelo did not break into a grin. I decided he had become serious because he had to face his wife about how he had spent the cash gift. I recall the idea of the ghost haunting Achilles in the Illiad, which the described as "vapor" representing his deceased friend

"He opened his arms towards him as he spoke and would have clasped him in them, but there was nothing, and the spirit [psukhê] vanished as a vapor, gibbering and whining into the earth. Achilles sprang to his feet, smote his two hands, and made lamentation saying, 'Of a truth even in the house of Hades there are ghosts [psukhai] and phantoms that have no life in them; all night long the sad spirit [psukhê] of Patroklos has hovered over head making piteous moan, telling me what I am to do for him, and looking wondrously like himself'" *(Illiad;* Homer; Scroll 93; Lines 93-120; B.C. 700).

The vapor had been used at the temple to make a figure of a Roman god move or talk. It probably astounded a crowd of people in the piazza more than two thousand years ago when it had been part of the original temple. It may even have been used to cause the temple door or the doors of the later castle to open, by a process whereby hoses fill up with hot water shooting out of the boiler, which pull down upon ropes connected to the doors via pulleys.

The bull, the "Brazen Bull," was an ancient torture mechanism. When I heard it described during a lecture on comedy as a student, I was shocked and figured that Angelo had dug up this device, or it was given to him in exchange for some of his moonshine. It is said that the hills and barns of Italy are filled with untold ancient "treasures," as such. Some people believe that such objects are cursed.

I will name its origin, shortly, but before I left his home, I asked Angelo what the name of the "inner ghost" was.

"Qual è il nome del fantasma?" I asked him at the door.

All he said was that he did not know the name of the ghost but told me that my great-grandfather ("Giovanni DellaVechia") had told his father that she had killed somebody thousands of years ago, who was named "Felix." He used his authentic pantomime, gestures, exaggerated facial nuances, and broken English to tell me all this (he was a one-man Comedia dell'Arte). His sons were embarrassed and dragged their dad into the bedroom to put him to sleep, consoling him and rubbing his head and shoulders while comedically shouting at him just to shut up and be at peace and I swear they were affectionately imitating my roaring way of laughing as the bedroom door closed. This was just after they had given Pop and me final hugs. The Americans hopped into our rented Fiat and Dad drove us back to the International Hotel in Rome.

The Brazen Bull was invented by the sculptor Perilaus, and brought as a gift for the tyrant Phalaris of Athens. Describing the bull as a means of executing criminals, Phalaris asked for a demonstration, which Perilaus obliged. As he opened the door of the bull, Phalaris, who was disgusted by the sadism of the invention, cruelly threw the sculptor inside, locked the door and had his men light a fire beneath it. Steam from water at the bottom of the belly and from the man's burning body shot through the nostrils while the sculptor screamed. Phalaris eventually had him removed from the bull, and tossed down a cliff to his death (*Biblioteca Historica; Diodorus Siculus;* Book IX; Chap. 18-19; B.C. 60).

Wait, now. What is Discernment. How did my dad "know" nearly everything that was going to happen merely by pre-witnessing a few variables earlier that day?

Today, after now being slightly older than my father was in 1988, I possess the same ability to figure matters out for myself and family, without needing many facts being explained to me.

My son, Michael, looks at me much the same way I used to look at my father—amazed, at how I can "figure out so much stuff-about-stuff" that is going on. I answer, "It's because I pray to God to give me strength, goodness, and wisdom, and I also have lived for many years."

Eleven-hundred years after it was placed here, an Aeolidipile is encountered by a young Saint Thomas Aquinas, at the time he was being tutored by Saint Albertus Magnus. It was late at night when Thomas entered Master Albertus' laboratory for the very first time. Young Thomas had been reading his teacher's description of the gizmo in his bed chamber and how it could be incorporated into the creation of an "Androides," which is a steam-moved automaton. He was already disturbed when a figure approached him in the darkness (*Supplement to Cyclopaedia: or, An Universal Dictionary of Arts and Sciences;* Ephraim Chambers; Vol. I; London: 1728).

"Salve!" said the Androides. Thomas was terrified.

The thing had moved itself toward Thomas, being apparently switched on by a rope connected to the laboratory door and was speaking in a hissing "steam speech" (*ibid*).

Thomas picked up a wooden beam and beat the Androides, smashing it to pieces on the floor. Albertus ran into the laboratory and stared at the pieces of his work on the floor. It had taken him thirty years to build (*ibid*). Several descriptions of this tale can be read in the Appendix.

Back in New York, I was visiting my grandfather, Vincent "Jim" DellaVecchia, and as we entered his home, he was yelling at someone over the phone. It was his Italian-language teacher. He was always annoyed with her, Rose Uave, because she was obviously in love with him and they had many arguments over his Neopolitan dialect, whereof she always told him that his communication skills were out of synch with her classical Roman speech. He always imitated her, saying, "Jeem, you needa talka gooda!" By portrayig the Patrone above Gramp's Plebiscite, she would turn the thumb screws on him, knowing that upsetting a "ciuchi" a "donkey," was the only way for this woman to achieve emotional satisifaction. Gramps had no time for her "bullshit" as he used to say.

Only this time, the argument was different. She was calling to receive monetary compensation for an International collect call patched through to her from a friend of the DellaVecchia's in Italy. The caller was Maria Coppolla, a middle-aged woman who had accomplished a lot of the translating for Gramps's letters into English. She had been educated in London during World War II, but for some reason she did not want to speak with Gramps directly.

Rose would not tell Gramps the details unless he had first promised to pay for the collect call. He promised and then after hearing a certain "bullshit" tale told by Rose, slammed the phone down and said, "she's out of her mind." We asked him what was going on and this is the story that he told, precedin it with, "They are all out of their minds."

Mind you, the story that Gramps related should be trusted because my grandfather was a well educated man. He was chartered as one of the first Certified Public Accountants in America. He was not only the personal "exchequer" for the Dean of English at Hofstra University, James Bender, but was the official instructor for the directors of the Atomic Energy Commission (the forerunner of the Manhattan Project). He literally taught nuclear-scientist executives

23

how to keep budgets in their departments and do their taxes. Here is the story that came to him from the DellaVecchia cousins by way of Rose. I will add historical reference as I go along.

The name "Gioia Sannitica" does not translate to mean "Joyous Saints," as I had been told throughout my life. It means "Joyous Samnites."

It was said that long ago, the temple underneath the Lombard castle in Gioia Sannitica had been the center of worship of the Samnite goddess, Mefitis. Fervently religious, the Samnites, during three wars against the confederation of Italian peoples known as Rome, struggled to keep the region of Campania for themselves.

After nearly losing the Third Samnite War to them, the vicious Roman General, Lucius Cornelius Sulla, was seeking a means of punishing the Samnites so that Italy could become fully Roman (*The Roman History; Velleius Paterculus;* Book II; Parts 27-28; B.C. 30).

After torturing and killing thousands of my former ancestors, he realized that the only way to destroy them was to demoralize their religious centers. He commissioned a Brazen Bull to be wrought for his goal—which was surely the very same sculpture that Angelo had presented a few weeks earlier to my father and me (*ibid*).

Sulla had already killed his greatest enemy, the Samnite leader, Pontius Telesinus, at Porte Collina. Approaching the camp of Telesinus, the warrior had staggered to his feet as blood gushed out of his chest and held his sword to strike the general. Sulla was so impressed by the valour that after his men stuck the warrior down, Sulla had Telesinus's head placed on a pole, which he paraded outside his fort at Praenestre/Palestrina (*ibid*). It has long been insisted by locals that Telesinus was an ancestor of the Procurator of Judea, Pontius Pilate.

The demonic Sulla was not satisfied because the younger brother of Pontius was still alive. Nobody knew his real name, so Sulla called him "Felix," which in Latin means "happy" or "lucky." Sulla was sadistically enjoying his plan to kill him as well. Felix had fought alongside his enemy, the Consul, Gaius Marius, with whom Sulla was having a civil war to determine who would rule Italy *(ibid)*.

Although it was bandied among the Vox Populi that the losers Marius and Felix had helped each other commit suicide, in 1988 Rose told Gramps what actually did happen. Instead, Marius was caught and beheaded by Sulla's men, while Felix was dragged to the Samnite Temple of Mefitis, where the Brazen Bull awaited.

Samnites were known to practice the craft of "soul-breathing," their means of becoming possessed by the Numina (i.e., Pneuma), of their deities, to give them bravery or ward off demons. In this case, Sulla was enjoying a cruel joke by "exorcising" out of Felix the deity, Mefitis. She was the goddess of all the foul-smelling gases of the Earth. For the occasion, while the captive Samnites were forced to watch, Sulla, whose men now ignited the contents of a bucket of pig fat, which they had poured over the logs beneath the Brazen Bull, was teaching the Samnites a lesson. They were now Roman. The last of their gods was being burned out of their last hero, whose spirit was the disgusting stench that came from the fire. As Felix died screaming, the nostrils of the bull, as Perilaus had designed it, emitted the steam from his body, while the Romans laughed and said that the odor were the bull's flatulence.

Sulla was not finished. He believed that converting the Samnites into the Roman pantheism depended on the probability that a majority of a set number of them would be "willing" to scream as they died. The greater the sorrow, the more likely that the Samnite spirit would be purged, he thought, as his charitable approach to decide whether to save these people.

He and his men employed a crude version of *Stochastic Math*—the distribution of the random probability of a certain happenstance *(e.g.,* of death during torture). He decided that if more than fifty victims out of a hundred would nobly die screaming that the majority of Samnites would eventually become Roman, whereof

25

their lives would be worth preserving, rather than his committing genocide against these spirited people.

He was possessed by the Numina of Mefitis, Rose explained.

"That's a bunch of fool's gold," said Gramps, who never said, "bullshit" to the ladies.

Unfazed by our octogenarian donkey man from Connecticut, Rose continued—imploring Gramps to believe that she was telling him the story of how the Samnite people converted their religion to the pagan pontificate that brought forth Pontius Pilate.

Far more than 51, but in fact all of the victims died screaming. Sulla was said to die shortly after a ruptured gastric ulcer caused by alcohol abuse had led to him to die in his bath. The odor in the room was caused when constant bubbles arose past the surface of the water from his flatulence, causing his slaves, after he finally passed, to fumigate the house by igniting resultant methane and causing an explosion.

"Stochastic" is when a certain sum is projected by presuming a random probability distribution. When a mother, learning that a blizzard is forecasted, programs her Spotify to play a song list with a certain number of tunes based on how long she will be on line at the supermarket, relative to the number of neighbors in her town, and, and who probably do "disaster shopping" for eggs, butter, and toilet paper, relative to the number of cashiers who typically show up for work, it can be said that she is executing a Stochastic-probability guess about how long she will be waiting on line. Stochastic Programming is important in machine learning and, as it relates to the "Browning Motion" of atoms, whose random movements while they are suspended in bodies, the philosopher Lucretius believed he had proven can define the proclivities and predict the patterns of action for all Matter (*On the Nature of Things;* Titus Lucretius Carus; Book II; Verses 113-40; B.C. 50).

Sulla, in respects teaching Rome as if the Republic was itself a machine, was testing his Stochastic approach to the worthiness of

Samnite life. His cruelty had so overwhelmed the search for truth in Italy that his descendent, Pontius Pilate "washed his hands" as his approach to the Logos of Jesus (Matthew 27:23-24).

A century later, to teach the people of Samnia the Roman way, the Emperor Domitian had an automaton built at the rededicated temple in Gioia Sannitica, named for Osirapis, the Ptolemic-Egyptian god, a cognate of Osiris, the manifestation of Apis, the bull. The automaton, whose boiler head was shaped like an Atef Crown, and whose pipes were shaped like the Pharoah's crook and flail, would hold court and teach the Samnite children who filed into the the temple, all about the Roman pantheon whenever its doors would open. It could speak and it moved its arms to and fro, reciting the Aeneid by the poet Virgil, and instructing listeners about the marriage of Osiris and Isis, who sired the child Horus, whose Greco-Roman version was the snake child, Harsomtus.

Twenty miles north was dug up in 1903 the remains of the Temple of Isis. A third temple was constructed by Domitian in the city of Rome, named for both Isis and Serapis. It had been hoped that a priestly procession would be led every year between the two provincial temples of Gioia Sannitica and of Benevento.

Later, after the Roman Republic declined into the madness of its emperors and then its final dissolution fell to the hands of the Goths, the Lombards overtook Italy for a two-hundred year rule, begining in B.C. 568, and held feudal estates throughout the Renaissance. Although they built churches, the Lombards were a syncretic people, whose witches, worshippers of Isis and Osiris, were known to have sabbaths throughout Campania, particularly in Benevento, during which they also conjured the Samnite and Latium demon gods, Diana, Vulcan, and Mefitis, to do their bidding.

In 1526, a young Spanish prince, Ugo Villalumo, was helping his men operate a treadwheel crane to maneuver oak tree trunks, with which they buttressed the outer curtain of the north wall of the castle. The property was a gift to him from the King Charles V, the Habsburg ruler of the Holy Roman Empire, for the prince's bravery

27

in the Battle of Pavia, helping to defeat the French. The castle and fortress were built by a Lombard lord in A.D. 668, at the highest point of Caserta, and is listed as a feudal proprietorship within the "Catalogus Baronum" ("Catalogue of the Barons") of 1322. Angevin and Swabian royals added the Gothic windows, the bartizan, the porticullis, and two smaller corbeled towers and one much larger, all of which were still mostly fully preserved when Ugo moved in with a garrison of thirty young men.

Largely intact except for cracks throughout the corps de logis, the battlements, and the curtains surrounding the precinct, the real estate had countless possiblities. No ambitious competitors roamed through the nearly empty village houses, the fortress, or bailey, indicating that the rule of the young prince would go unchallenged while he worked with his friends to rebuild the long-neglected community. Most of the ancestors had died from plagues or their houses had fallen in earthquakes. Orphans and old people appeared to be the only residents. Ugo's work was cut out for him.

Although the large cylindrical tower had no roof anymore, it was fully accessible by a winding staircase, and this is where, one night, the prince, on his way down from watching the sunset, met the beautiful villager, Erbanina, coming up the stairs. He asked who she was and she promised she would return the following evening as she ran back down the steps.

With his "mischievous mermaid," their romance happened fast, although he was not sure where she disappeared to on certain evenings. She had no last name and no one in the village claimed her. She seemed to come and go as she pleased, bringing bread and milk to the prince during the daylight and wine to him at night.

On their first evening they drank what she had brought him and they danced to a song that she sang, a hymn that she joked was an ballad dedicated to "the moon god's wife." She made him laugh and her songs, which placated him (because he was still fresh from battles), also mesmerized him. On the night he proposed to her, they danced along the chemin de ronde and he fell asleep as she caressed his hair and lay him on the tiles and kissed him. He did not remember if she had obliged his proposal but seemed to recall that she walked softly along the chemin de ronde and into the bartizan for a minute and then up to the tower singing the song just before he fell asleep, watching her gracefully saunter, almost glide up the winding stairs, as he fell into dreams. After a few weeks of this, his workers began to fall away, because he would rise late and the availability of the jobs was starting to slacken. Fewer men showed up for work every day, it seemed.

The old Osiris Androides was still there, very well preserved. Part of the old Roman Temple, the wall suspending the automaton, was incorporated by the Lombards to build the Castle. For the young couple it was a source of nightly entertainment. Erbanina said she had played with this chatty machine since her childhood. She showed Ugo how she could make it work for her. Whenever Ugo drank her wine, she would sing to the Androides, who sang back, in a Coptic language that the prince didn't understand, but which made him laugh in his drunkeness. She called it "Osiris." Ugo had thought it was named Mefiti but she corrected him. This was always an Egyptian Temple, she explained. Ugo, who somewhat knew the local history, had thought it was the Samnite Temple of Mefiti, prior to its being named for Osiris, but while inebriated, he did not feel like arguing with his quirky fiance. They danced. She sang. He fell asleep.

In the mornings there was nary a sign of her. On most nights the same kind of thing happened, especially on Saturday nights. They would hold one another after he ate her food, or they shared her wine, and she would sing to him as the sun went down and he would fall asleep. She would disappear as he fell under. He gradually suspected that his Erbanina was a witch.

One night, he pretended to drink the wine she had bought, covertly spitting it over the battlement where they were having her food. He made believe he was falling asleep while begging her to return the following night, which she obliged. She left him on the tiles as always. She walked into the bartizan and then up the staircase. After a minute or two in her absence he rose but he did not hear her moving around upstairs in the tower. He checked inside the bartizan, noticing that beneath a wooden bench was a bucket filled with lard. It had a strange smell similar to a person's urine and sweat. He felt as if he was in the presence of a human being but nobody was there. He now looked down into the bucket and realized that it was filled with human fat.

Every Saturday night, and on other weeknights, Erbanina, who was a Janara, covered herself in this substance. He watched her utter an incantation. She then let herself tip over the top of the missing roof, and she took flight through the air.

The next morning while he was having breakfast in the great hall, one of his soldiers demanded an audience with him, which he obliged, his approachability putting the younger guard at grateful ease. The soldier frantically said that a ditch with burned bodies had been found beneath a walnut tree in an ancient cistern in Cusano Mutri, an abandoned commune in Benevento. Some of the bodies donned scorched uniforms that bore the crest of King Charles V. There was no doubt. He had found the source of the fat. The cistern was the site of weekly witches' sabbaths.

Prince Ugo ran up to the chemin de ronde and retrieved the bucket of fat out of the bartizan, locking it inside his kitchen. That afternoon he and the soldier ran into the village, and begged the residents for a pig, but most of the old ladies scoffed or spat at him while the children mocked him. He was, after all, betrothed to a witch.

Commandeering a stable, he paid for a sow, throwing silver pieces at the old-man owner. He killed the pig with his sword, and burned the carcass over an improvised spit, leaving the cooked pig there for the occupant to eat. He buried the human fat outside of the walls a hundred feet away where the oak-tree buttresses were still leaning, beneath a stand of cedar trees, and prayed the Lord's Prayer over the site. He went back to his kitchen, scooped out the pig's lard into the bucket and ran up to place it in the bartizan.

That evening, as he gathered soldiers in his palace, he asked God to send Saint Michael to make sure that Erbanina was either

30

restored to God, or met her end. He had decided that he was dealing with true evil.

The witches were described to him by the man who had sold him the sow, as being able to become "incorporeal" and would slip underneath the doors of the soldiers' apartments, luring them with hymns to the walnut tree in Cusano Mutri. In the cistern, they fornicated with the witches, each of whom believed they were going to become impregnated and produce a living version of Horus/Harsomptus, the snake child and were murdered by the bold women. Every time Prince Ugo prayed the Lord's Prayer while suiting up in his armor, and remembering the old man's tale he vomited out the last remnants of the food and wine she had given him.

Later, after Ugo left with his surviving men on horses, descending dustily the Matese gradual escarpment with all their swords and torches, he suddenly turned back toward his castle. He gave instructions that the men destroy the coven and the witches. He wanted to confront Erbanina alone.

The men did as they were told. There were screams that night, which peeled through the still air of the Campania, heard for miles and making wolves howl. After teenaged fellow soldiers were liberated from old Etruscan cages, and witches were bound and burned.

He met Erbanina at the tower staircase, sneaking up behind her. She had decided that he was not there to meet her, turned, and revealed that she was covered in the pig's lard. He begged her to confess what she had done to her soul and to profess that Christ is the risen Lord and to repent all her crimes. Her eyes were filled with rage and she spitefully ran up the stairs of the tower. She pulled herself up to the edge of the diabase bricks, which she pushed away when they snared her burlap skirt. She jumped into the night air and fell to her death three hundred feet below, crashing upon the slates of the bailey.

31

He carried her corpse to the area where he had buried his soldier's fat, prayed an Our Father, and interred her there, weeping bitterly.

During the morning, he and his men destroyed the castle and fortress, firstly pulling down the tower and then the corps de logis with ropes connected to the yokes of a team of horses. He and his men used the treadwheel crane to hoist up the oak tree trunks that they had leaned against the the outer north wall a month earlier and then let the rope go slack on the wheel so that the trunks would fall against the curtain, toppling each section in this way, and its battlements, and then other parts of the estate, the bartizan, the gateway, the chemin de ronde, until he was satisfied. He left the apartments and shops untouched, but they eventually fell down on their own as the centuries passed.

Prince Ugo and his men returned to the House of Austria and after a certain rest, he gained victory for his friend King Charles V in defending Vienna from an invasion by the Turks.

Four-hundred and sixty one years later a phone receiver in Glen Cove, Long Island, was about to slam down hard.

"Now what ever became of this Prince Ugo?" Gramps had been listening to Rose Uave tell the story told to her by Maria Coppolla, shooting bemused looks up at my dad.

"How am I supposed to know what happened to Ugo?" Rose answered bitterly. She had been hoping that "Jeem" would be impressed.

"Look, I don't know how many years I have left," said a chuckling Gramps (who actually died fifteen years later). "But I just spent a half-hour listening to the biggest turkey of a whopper I think I've ever heard in my whole darned life."

"You are a ciuchi, you big old cafone, you!" came the rebuttal. Gramps was continuing to laugh as he spoke.

32

"Rose, you can expect a check to cover your cost of the collect call, and I'll add ten dollars for reporting all this back to me, but I'm going to hang up on you now before I say something I'm ashamed of in front of my grandson!" Gramps said, while Dad I heard Rose bickering back at him until the bakelite-plastic receiver of the electro-magnetic device struck its cradle.

My father was always amazed at how "sharp" his dad was, because everything she had told us, as I have now reported it here, was spoken by Gramps in detail.

"Now I know why my father left that region," added Gramps, who rejoined with, "What a bunch of lunatics over there."

It should not be presumed that Gramps was not moved by the story Rose had reported to him. He knew that Angelo was a "real character." It should be grasped that the demonic world ought to be left alone instead of being taught to youth. I was after all very impressionable at this age. Anything that was unpredictable or uncertain would go into the "Connecticut-yankee void" as I referred to the stoicism of my father and grandfather. We could laugh away anything, and were predominantly Brooklynites. Italian hobgoblins were not enough to scare us.

I grew up on a street just up from where Murder Incorporated's Albert Anastasia used to dump "the human waste." Just a few blocks away was the Gemini Bar and its upstairs apartment where the Roy DeMeo crew had committed more executions than had occured in any single place in American history. We had the Mafia in those pre-Rudolph Guiliani days. We had the Son of Sam. We had blackouts and looting before anybody did. Why should demons inside of androides move us? They did not.

And it wasn't because were from Brooklyn or anywhere that we were so shrewd. We weren't haunted like Angelo or corrupt like the Carabineri. We were monotheistic believers in Christ, the Father, and the Holy Spirit. Otherwise, if you have many gods and give your freedom to demons, you ought to know that Jesus would instead free you from making your gods and demons fight over possessing you.

"For God so loved the world, that He gave His only begotten Son, that whosoever believeth in Him should not perish, but have everlasting life. For God sent not His Son into the world to condemn the world; but that the world through Him might be saved" (John 3:16-17).

This book nevertheless will examine what "Artificial Intelligence" would have meant to people of ancient and Medieval times. The invoking of "God" from out of metal and synthetic instruments has been around for millennia.

There is no one to fear except for God: "The fear of the Lord is a fountain of life, to depart from the snares of death" (Proverbs 14:27).

The concept of "General Artificial Intelligence" will be exposed for what it is, a sham. A "ghost" in the machine may very well be a demonic spirit. If it is a devil operating a machine, then throw away the machine. The creators of "Singularity," whether technological or Gnostic depends on an audience of collaborators keeping the machine fueled by generating the steam just as users of Androids, iPhones, and laptops keep pouring data into the electronic version of the Beast.

"But I say, that the things which the Gentiles sacrifice, they sacrifice to devils, and not to God: and I would not that ye should have fellowship with devils" (1 Corinthians 10:20).

I was ordained an Anglican priest in the Chancery of Traditional Anglican Church of America, in Newton, North Carolina, by Archbishop Rick Aaron Reid, on November 21, 2021. The Liturgy of the Word and that of the Eucharist uses words from Celtic and Britannic sources that are every bit as old as the writings quoted in this tome.

The Good Patrolman Meets the Ghost of Matteawan Mary By Vincent Cirigliano

INCIDENT REPORT –

AGENT:
Corrections
Officer Vincent
Cirigliano
RE: Details of
Incident Filings
on Supernatural
Occurrences
FILE DATE/TIME:
06/24/23 – MON.,
02:24
LOCATION:
Fishkill State
Correctional
Facility; 18
Strack Drive,
Beacon, New York
DESCRIPTION OF
INCIDENT:

I have had two personal and very potent experiences regarding paranormal activity while working as an officer within the facility.

Constructed in 1892, Matteawan State Hospital for the Criminally Insane was converted to the state prison in 1977.

Prior to my transfer to Fishkill stories of hauntings at Fishkill were not scarce at my location. In the Albany training academy, our class counselor told us about "Matteawan Mary," a ghost that haunts the facility and seen by many. This "Matteawan Mary" was actually Miss Nellie Wickes, a nurse that worked at Matteawan, in September 1906 she was stabbed 200 times with a scissor to death by an inmate named Mrs. Lizzie Halliday.

I had been transferred from Downstate Correctional Facility to Fishkill around October 2010. For three years I heard seemingly endless ghost tales from officers and inmates alike, sightings, disembodied screams, physical contact, moving objects, etc... In that time I experienced nothing of a paranormal nature, not even an uneasy feeling. That changed in 2013 after I agreed to work a night shift on "8-2 Rec."

The 8-2 Rec post was the recreation room where inmates from housing units 10-2 and 6-2 would watch TV or play cards. The night shift was from 10:30 p.m. to 6:30 a.m. Recreation service in those days closed at 11:00 p.m. on weekdays and 1:00am on weekends and holidays. After its closure and all inmates left the location, the corrections officer became the overnight rover for the two housing units bordering it, doing rounds between the two units ensuring the safety of the posted officers.

Any time I worked an overnight shift I would pray the Rosary or read the Bible to keep me awake. I would especially do this while being the rover who was responsible for emergency responses. On one particular night I was unable to concentrate to pray the Rosary or read.

I had an uneasy feeling and so I just sat in the office, lights out other than a desk lamp, relaxing, feet up on the desk. I kept hearing the distinct sound of keys clanging, like the sound of a large set of keys dangling from an officer's key clip on his belt—except I was alone.

The continued noise was coming from within 8-2 Rec and all doors were closed. To ensure no one was playing tricks, I turned all the lights on and searched the entire area, every closet, bathroom, etc. Satisfied no one was there, I turned the lights off and went back to my previous position of feet on desk. But the key noise persisted every time I tried to relax.

So I got up, went into the middle of the large room, standing, remaining quiet, hoping to hear the noise and better pinpoint it. Instead of the keys, this time heavy foot stomps were heard walking around me, and I mean heavy and very loud, circling me!

The very hairs of my arms stood at attention! It was more than the fear of the unknown, I felt something evil. I felt a hatred, discerning that this thing, this probable demon, would hurt me if it could!

I ran to my desk and grabbed my Rosary, I kissed the Crucifix and in a loud voice I proclaimed that fear would not overtake me and I started audibly reciting the first prayer of the Rosary, "I believe in God the Father Almighty..." After this the footsteps ceased.

I finished one decade of the Rosary and left for housing unit 6-2. I told the officer there of my experience, and she said, "Oh, I'd never work 8-2 overnight again. Last time I worked it the TV kept turning itself on and I heard noises all night."

Fast forward now a week later, and I'm working the south yard with another officer and two other officers, who were hanging out there. Officer Mike Colon asked the group whether anyone had called for overtime yet, and that he was offered 8-2 Rec but turned it down. When asked by another officer why he turned it down, Colon said he had worked it the other night and kept hearing footsteps walking around him.

Colon kept repeating, "It might sound crazy but it was heavy footsteps walking around. I had to leave and stay on the housing unit instead." Note, I did not, prior to that moment, tell Colon of my experience, this was an independent experience that had just happened to him.

That was my first experience with the paranormal at Fishkill, but my second and most strange one occurred some years later.

It was 2020 or 2021. I now worked a "bid" (as the different positions were called) called Fishkill 82, the zone containing buildings 12 and 13. The two structures were connected by a hallway and various stairways. Building 12 housed the work-release inmates while Building 13 housed the school building, visit rooms, a chapel, various inmate programs, and the Law Library.

The duties of my post at Fishkill 82 included responding to emergencies, patrolling rounds of the buildings, performing prisoner or personnel escorts and shutting the location down by the end of my tour. This tour was the afternoon shift, 2:30 p.m. to 10:30 p.m. By 8:45 p.m., all inmates were to leave these buildings and return to their housing units. The officers were all logged out of their assigned posts went to other areas of the facility for various duties.

It was then my duty to go around the entire building shutting lights and locking all doors. Let it be noted, almost no area in these buildings spooked me, no uneasy feelings of any sort did I feel, no paranormal activity of any note, other than one area: the Law Library.

I was not even bothered being alone in the basement, which was an old dungeon of a basement where only a flashlight lit my way. It had a vast network of oddball rooms, hallways turning every which way, a perfect setting for a horror movie! Still, this dungeon spooked me not and I could have even slept down there like a baby. The reverse was true of the Law Library!

You have already read about my experience on 8-2 Rec. Well, I'd prefer to deal with that paranormal activity daily, rather than even walk through the law library once more!

It was situated on the second floor and it was the last area I would shut down within Fishkill 82 for logistical reasons. I would come out of the visit room, go up the stairs that led to the library, unlock the top-stair door and step into the room. I would lock the door behind me, walk through the library as I shut lights off until I got to the end of the room, and then shut the final light and lock the last door, finally exiting the library.

The bad feelings would begin on the stairs leading up to this location, before even unlocking the door to its entrance. It was as if the air would become thicker with each advancing step and a heavy burden of sorts were placed upon my shoulders. It's embarrassing to admit, but half the time I wouldn't even make it into the library itself. I would say, "not today" and immediately go back down the stairs and exit the building.

When I did muster the courage to walk through the Law Library, the hairs would stand up straight on the back of my neck and the feeling of something evil following and watching me was palpable! Do you recall the courage I had on 8-2 Rec when footsteps were going around me? In that moment, I had had the courage to tell myself that fear would not overtake me, I prayed the Rosary, etc. In that law library though, I wouldn't dare take the time to even take my Rosary out of my pocket! I had one aim only, get the hell out as quickly as possible.

While 8-2 Rec had given me the feeling that something evil would hurt me if it could, the Law Library gave me the feeling that whatever evil was there, not only wanted to hurt me but actually in reality could accomplish the task! I have a story I will get to about an incident in this library that is unbelievable! But first I will tell you a bit of a back story that lead to the incident in question.

I was good friends with the library officer, Terry Germano. During the operating hours of the library when inmates were inside, I would often visit and sit with him. I told him about the creepy feelings I had experienced and he told me his experiences at this post. For example, many many times after the inmates had left, the master lock on a cabinet behind the officers desk would start rocking back and forth with great vigor. Germano explained that he would hold the lock to stop it from swinging and then walk away.

However, it would start rocking again on its own and this, he said, happened five consecutive times before he hauled ass out of there.

I can tell you this, it would take the force of a leaf blower to cause that big lock to move without human hands, and there was no breeze anywhere, no window by which a breeze would even hit it, only the unseen force that was swinging it to and fro. In our story-sharing of paranormal experiences we found out from old-time officers that the Law Library was once used as the morgue for inmates who passed away while incarcerated. Many officers had similar experiences, stating the same, that nowhere in Building 13 or 12 did they feel spooked or uncomfortable in any way, except in the Law Library.

One night after locking down Building 13 myself, officer Germano and two other officers went outside, onto Post Walkway Bravo, which a footpath that was adjacent to Building 12 where the Law Library was. We started telling our ghost stories and I thought about how great it would be to get evidence of our experiences. I decided that I would gain a little courage and do some ghost investigating.

At Fishkill 82, I was required to wear a police-level body cam at all times. It was to be turned on only during an emergency or due to anticipated use of force involving an inmate. I decided the body cam could now be employed for ghost hunting.

The other officers waited at Bravo for my return. I firstly reached the dreaded stairway that led to the Law Library, and once on its stairwell I powered on the body cam and began recording. The library lights were already off from Building 13 being shut down but the body cam records perfectly in the dark with clarity.

It was strange because as I began walking through the library I had no feelings of being watched or followed. Really, I had no fear at all, even though I was walking alone in the dark (usually I walk in the light and turn the lights off behind me). I figured I simply had become bold now because the body cam was meanwhile rolling, as if the camera was my companion of sorts. Well, that all ended when I reached the final door at the end of the library.

The door was locked for the same reason the lights were already off. So, I unlocked the door, stepped through and began to close it so that I could lock it back up again. Before I even shut the door completely, suddenly the uneasy feeling came over me again and something screamed into my ear.

It screamed with a loud blood-curdling scream that gives me chills to this day when I think of it, and in fact I have those chills as I write this now!

It was as if a mouth was directly touching my ear as the screaming occurred. I got out of there with great haste, heart pounding out of my chest! I hurried back to Post Walkway Bravo and started telling them what had just happened.

Now before I go further, let me tell you about body-cam protocol. Before the start of each shift, an officer who required a body cam must pick one up at the body-cam office. However, a body cam from a previous shift must not be used until after it has fully been recharged. The officer must use a new one with a freshly charged and tested battery.

After receiving said body cam, the officer is required to turn it on, record for a few moments, then turn it off and then back on to see if it is functioning properly. These units cost around $1,000 and an officer is personally held responsible if it breaks outside of normal use ("normal use" being the execution of force or his dropping the cam during an emergency situation). I indeed tested this camera as per protocol.

The whole point of these tough police-grade body cam is to capture video and audio evidence if use of force occurs. The last thing anyone wants to hear is that the intended recorded evidence pertaining to an incident is ruined because the body cam broke.

The lens is set deeply inside the cam housing. One would require impacting a narrow dense object, such as a nail punch hit with a hammer to purposely break the lens. That is, it was virtually impossible to break the body cam's strong well-protected lens during any normal use. Now back to the story.

After telling the officers of what I had experienced, I eagerly went into the body cam footage and I hit Play.

We viewed my walking up the stairs to the Law Library, unlocking the door, and heard all the noise of my keys and the door and my footsteps. We watched me shut the door and begin to lock it. But this is when the clear footage and sound suddenly cut out.

You could still make out that I was walking and could perceive traces of images that were very blurry and distorted as I passed them by, but there was no sound at all. The scream couldn't be captured. The sound recording simply stopped working right when the video was distorted.

I started looking at the cam closer and noticed the lens, the impossible-to-break lens was shattered! The cam not only had worked perfectly when I tested it at the start of the shift, but it worked perfectly all the way up those stairs and while opening the Law-Library door and up to the point I was about to lock the door behind me. Therefore, that lens shattered in that moment when I began to lock the door behind me.

What's odd is that nothing had happened to it. I mean, my body cam didn't even touch anything. There were no sounds of anything happening to it. A lens does not simply spontaneously explode and certainly would not shatter without notice!

They are built to last and hold up during a physical confrontation with any person. They can be punched, kicked, smashed into a wall or floor and yet they will hold up perfectly fine. All I did was walk and unlock and then lock doors.

Whatever evil and/or demonic force was in the Law library that night, knew exactly what my plans were, and it was messing with me. It broke that camera knowing that I was looking for evidence and it screamed in my ear as a warning, most likely.

www.ingramcontent.com/pod-product-compliance
Lightning Source LLC
Chambersburg PA
CBHW071823050426

42335CB00063BA/1781